THE UNTAMED WORLD

Kangaroos

Patricia Miller-Schroeder

RAINTREE
Steck-Vaughn
RSVP **PUBLISHERS**

A Harcourt Company

Austin   New York
www.raintreesteckvaughn.com

Published by Raintree Steck-Vaughn Publishers, an imprint of Steck-Vaughn Company.

Library of Congress Cataloging-in-Publication Data

Miller-Schroeder, Patricia.
   Kangaroos / Patricia Miller-Schroeder.
      p. cm. -- (The untamed world)
   Includes bibliographical references (p.).
   Summary: Describes the physical characteristics, behavior, and habitat of different species of kangaroos, presents their place in Australian folklore, and discusses some of the threats they face.
   ISBN 0-7398-4972-7
      1. Kangaroos--Juvenile literature. [1. Kangaroos.] I. Title. II. Series.

   QL737.M35 M55 2002
   599.2'22--dc21

                                        2001048364

Printed and bound in Canada
1234567890 05 04 03 02 01

Project Coordinator
Heather Kissock
Editor
Lauri Seidlitz
Raintree Steck-Vaughn Editor
Simone T. Ribke
Copy Editor
Diana Marshall
Illustration and Layout
Warren Clark
Bryan Pezzi
Photo Research
Joe Nelson

Consultants
David Croft, School of Biological Science, University of New South Wales, Sydney, Australia

Helen Robertson, Curator of Australian Fauna, Perth Zoo, Perth, Australia

Acknowledgments
The publisher wishes to thank Warren Rylands for inspiring this series.

Contents

Introduction

When people think of Australian animals, they often think of koalas or kangaroos.

Opposite: In Australia, kangaroos are often just called "'roos."

When people think of Australian animals, they often think of koalas or kangaroos. Both koalas and kangaroos belong to a group of animals called **marsupials**. Marsupials give birth to young that are not fully formed. These newborns must grow and develop for many months before they can live apart from their mother. Many marsupials, such as the kangaroo, carry their young in a pouch until they become fully developed.

In this book you will meet kangaroos that are no larger than a rat and others that look like rabbits. You will see kangaroos that live in trees, swamps, and rock piles. You will learn how some kangaroos can live in deserts so dry that there is no water for most of the year. You will discover how a young kangaroo keeps from falling out of its mother's pouch when she hops around. Turn the page and meet this amazing family of animals.

There are over 40 species of kangaroos in Australia. Wallabies make up one group of kangaroos.

Features

All kangaroos are marsupials and carry their young in pouches.

Opposite: A kangaroo's pouch is formally called a marsupium.

The continent of Australia is very large and has many different habitats in which animals can live. Kangaroos have developed special features that help them survive in these varied habitats. Many kangaroos live in dry areas and have features that help them conserve water. Others live in forests and need to climb trees or hide in shrubs to avoid predators. Some kangaroos have features that help them travel on rock piles as safely as mountain goats.

Yet, all kangaroos share some of the same special features. All kangaroos are marsupials and carry their young in pouches. Scientists call kangaroos **macropods** because they have big feet, *macro* meaning "large" and *pod* meaning "foot" in Greek. Kangaroos travel on two sturdy hind legs, and most travel by hopping. What other kangaroo features can you see in the photograph on this page? Read on to discover how these features help the kangaroo live and thrive.

A kangaroo hopping across the countryside is a common sight in Australia.

Australia's Marsupials

Many millions of years ago, all of Earth's land masses were joined together. Slowly, over millions of years, large chunks of land began to drift apart, eventually forming today's continents. Around 100 to 150 million years ago, the pieces of land that are now Antarctica, Africa, South America, India, and Australia started to break up. First Africa and India separated. Then South America broke away from Antarctica. Finally, around 45 to 65 million years ago, Australia broke free of Antarctica and drifted north.

Marsupial **mammals** likely evolved in North America about 85 million years ago. Over time, many other types of animals developed and moved into the areas already inhabited by marsupials. These new animals were better adapted to the area than the marsupials and gradually forced them to move further south. The marsupials moved throughout South America and as far as Australia, on Antarctica's far end.

In most of the world, the other animals eventually took over. This left only a few marsupials in South America that managed to survive. Before the newer animals could migrate as far south as Australia, the continent had broken free and was no longer connected to other pieces of land. The Australian marsupials were separated from the other animals by large bodies of water. They were free to develop without competition. These marsupials were the ancestors of Australia's unique group of marsupial animals.

At one time, the continents were one huge land mass, and animals could move from land to land freely.

Kangaroo Ancestors

Small rat-sized marsupials that lived in trees about 25 million years ago were likely the first kangaroo ancestors. These small creatures eventually came out of the trees to explore other habitats. By 8 million years ago, many kangaroo species began to get larger. Some lived in groups on Australia's spreading grasslands.

Some of the earlier kangaroos became giants. About 2 million years ago, a kangaroo called *Procoptodon goliah* stood over 9 feet (2.7 m) tall and weighed 500 pounds (227 kg). It became extinct about 40,000 years ago. *Procoptodon goliah* may have disappeared because of changes to its habitat. It is also possible that humans may have hunted it to extinction. Early hunters

often preferred to hunt larger animals to get more meat for their efforts. About 50 species of large Australian animals disappeared due to hunting by humans. Over the past 40,000 years, the size of kangaroos has been steadily shrinking. Kangaroos today are about 30 percent smaller than their ancestors. Some scientists believe that this decrease in size has occurred as a defense against these early hunters and their desire for large animals.

In terms of size, rat kangaroos most resemble the early ancestors of today's kangaroos.

Size

Members of the kangaroo family can be both large and small. Small kangaroo species, such as the rat kangaroo, weigh less than 2 pounds (0.9 kg). Red kangaroos are the largest species. Red kangaroo males can stand over 7 feet (2.1 m) tall and weigh 200 pounds (90 kg). Many of the large kangaroo species, such as the red and grey kangaroos, have large size differences between males and females. Females may be only half the size of the bigger males. Kangaroos grow throughout their life, which means that the largest males are also the oldest.

No matter how large kangaroos grow, they all start life as very tiny creatures. Large species of kangaroos have tiny newborns that are only about three-quarters of an inch (1.9 cm) long. This is the size of a large bee. Small species have even smaller newborns.

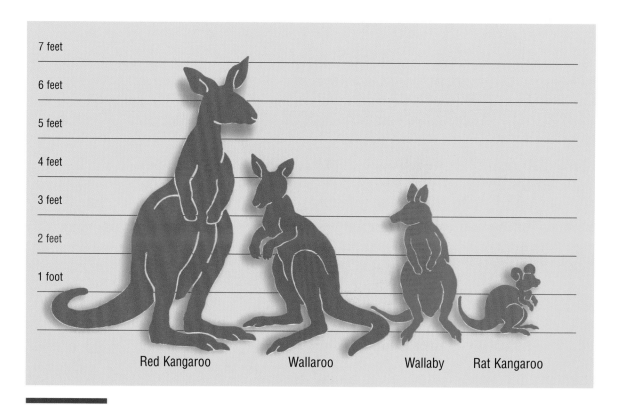

Kangaroos range in size from the very large to the very small.

Hair and Color

Kangaroos are mammals and, like other mammals, their bodies are covered with hair. Newborn kangaroos are pink and hairless. Their fur grows as they develop in the pouch. Most species' skin will be covered by a fur coat between 3 and 6 months of age. Many kangaroos are shades of blue, gray, or red, but some are black, yellow, or brown. Patterns of stripes, splotches, or rings of different colors dress up some kangaroo coats. Males and females of the same species can often be different colors. Male red kangaroos are usually red. Female red kangaroos can be red or gray. In different habitats, there can even be gray males and red females. This size and color difference has fooled some people into thinking that the males and females are different species!

Fur color varies in kangaroos. Some have very dark fur, while the fur of others can be almost white.

LIFE SPAN

Most of the information on how long kangaroos can live comes from the better-known species, such as the red and grey kangaroos. Six or seven years is an average life span for a kangaroo in the wild. However, some kangaroos can live to be about 20 years old. Kangaroos that reach an old age are limited by how long their teeth last. A kangaroo's molar teeth wear out from eating tough plant food and are naturally replaced one at a time. The limit for tooth replacement is 16 molar teeth, so old kangaroos can run out of teeth.

Special Adaptations

Kangaroos have many special features that help them to survive in their natural environments in Australia.

Legs for Leaping

Kangaroos are excellent hoppers, due mainly to special adaptations in their legs and feet. Kangaroo hind legs are large and powered by strong muscles. Kangaroos have almost twice as much muscle as other animals their size. Even when standing still, their legs are bent and ready to hop. When they jump, powerful muscles attached to elastic-like **tendons** pull on the leg bones. The legs straighten out to full length, and the kangaroo leaps forward. Other muscles pull the leg bones back into a fold to prepare for another leap. Once a kangaroo gets going, it can hop for a long time without tiring. A leap of 27 feet (8.2 m) is not unusual for a large kangaroo.

When necessary, the largest kangaroos can jump over 10-foot (3 m) fences from a standing position. Bushes and rocks are not obstacles, either. Bouncing helps kangaroos escape from predators, such as **dingoes**. Although many people believe that kangaroos cannot move their legs separately, this is not the case. Kangaroos are excellent swimmers and can even shuffle backward. Both activities require independent movement of the back legs.

At cruising speed, kangaroos travel at about 20 miles per hour (32 km/h). They can hop at speeds of up to 40 miles per hour (60 km/h), if necessary.

The long toes on the kangaroo's hind feet play an important role in the takeoff of a hop.

Big Feet

Another feature that helps a kangaroo hop is its big feet. Kangaroo hind feet are long and thin. They provide a springboard from which to push off for each leap. Most kangaroos have four toes on each hind foot. Each toe has a sharp claw. The middle toe is extra long and does much of the work when pushing into a jump. It is also a weapon. Male kangaroos often use this middle claw during fights with other males or in defense against predators. The two innermost toes are joined. These fused toes provide kangaroos with a handy comb that they use to remove dirt from their fur. Kangaroos have five clawed toes on their smaller front feet. These toes are also used in fights and grooming.

Tails

Tails are important tools in helping animals keep their balance. A kangaroo's tail is almost as long as the rest of its body. It is also loaded with muscles. A large male kangaroo can balance its entire body weight on its tail when fighting. The male will lean back on his tail and kick at his opponent with both hind legs at the same time. When a kangaroo is hopping fast, it will stretch its tail out behind it and tip it slightly upward. This balances the kangaroo's body. The tail keeps the kangaroo from tipping forward. It can even help the kangaroo change direction in mid-air.

The tail has one other important function. It helps the kangaroo walk. Kangaroos' legs are great for speed, but not as good for walking or moving slowly. For large kangaroos the tail provides support, like a big extra leg. The kangaroo places all four feet on the ground, with its tail drawn in close behind. It then supports its body on its forefeet and tail while both hind legs are swung forward. The kangaroo then squats on its hind legs and shuffles forward on its forefeet and tail. This slow, awkward method of getting around is used while the kangaroo is feeding or socializing. Smaller kangaroos drag their tails.

More Special Adaptations

Teeth

Kangaroos have a space behind their front teeth where they form plant material into wads. These wads of tough plant material are then ground up by big teeth called molars. Over time the kangaroos' molar teeth wear out and are replaced by new ones. A kangaroo mouth is much like a conveyor belt. The molar teeth grow in the back of the mouth and slowly move forward. By the time one tooth is completely worn out, it has reached the front of the mouth and falls out. A new molar takes its place, offering a fresh grinding surface. A kangaroo will produce about 16 molar teeth during its lifetime.

Sight and Hearing

Kangaroos are nocturnal. Nocturnal means that animals are more active at night than they are in the day. Because they are nocturnal, kangaroos have to be able to see when there is not much light. Like other nocturnal animals, they have developed eyes that take in as much light as possible.

Kangaroos have large ears that are like those of a deer. The ears can be turned in all directions and can pick up sounds from great distances. They help warn kangaroos of any approaching danger.

With their keen senses of sight, smell, and hearing, kangaroos are alert to their surroundings.

Female kangaroos clean their pouches as part of their grooming ritual.

Pouches

Pouches are a special adaptation that allows kangaroos to raise their infants in a safe place. This is an important feature for animals that live in environments where they must travel long distances to find food and where they have to travel quickly to avoid predators. Special pouch features include a milk source that provides food for young, and special muscles that can close the pouch against danger. A pouch with a big infant inside can be heavy. Both male and female kangaroos have special bones in their pelvis to help support the weight. However, only female kangaroos develop a pouch to carry and nourish the young.

Temperature Regulation

Red kangaroos have developed ways of surviving in hot, dry environments. When humans and most other animals get too hot, they cool down by sweating. Kangaroos need to save water, so they only sweat when they are active. For this reason, kangaroos are usually not very active during the day, when the temperature is hottest. This helps them save water. Kangaroos, like dogs, also pant and drool. This helps them cool down when air passes rapidly over their moist tongue and mouth.

Classification

Kangaroos are mammals, like dogs, tigers, deer, and humans. They belong to the large group of mammals called marsupials. While some marsupials live in South America, New Guinea, and islands surrounding Australia, most call Australia home. There are between 53 and 69 species of kangaroos. Experts do not always agree on exactly how many kangaroo species there are. Some species are very rare, and some have just been discovered!

All animals have a scientific name so that scientists from different countries can understand each other's work. The scientific names for the kangaroos listed on the next four pages are shown in parentheses. They come from Latin and Greek words.

True Kangaroos (*Macropodidae*)

Size is the main difference between various species in this family. Most look very similar, otherwise. True kangaroos live in a variety of habitats, from deserts, scrubs, and open plains to woodlands and moist forests. Members of the macropod family usually eat grasses and leaves.

Large Kangaroos

This group includes the largest and best-known of the kangaroos. They are widespread species that can weigh up to 200 pounds (90 kg). The red kangaroo (*Macropus rufus*) lives in dry environments such as deserts, scrubs, and grasslands in western and central Australia. A scrub environment is made up of small trees and shrubs. Both the eastern grey kangaroo (*Macropus giganteus*) and the western grey kangaroo (*Macropus fuliginosus*) are common in many parts of east, south, and southwest Australia.

The western grey is the kangaroo most adaptable to different climates.

Wallaroos

Wallaroos are midway between the large kangaroos and wallabies in size. Some big males can weigh up to 110 pounds (50 kg), but females are much smaller. There are three species of wallaroos. The common wallaroo (*Macropus robustus*) is often called the euro. It is widespread in habitats from dry grasslands to coastal rain forests. The antilopine wallaroo (*Macropus antilopinus*) lives in the rain forests of northern Australia.

The antilopine wallaroo is a highly social animal and can be found in groups of various sizes.

Wallabies

Wallabies are small kangaroos. Full grown adults usually weigh less than 44 pounds (20 kg). Some experts decide that a kangaroo is a wallaby if its hind feet are shorter than 10 inches (25.4 cm). The several types of wallabies are the macropod, swamp, hare, nail-tail, rock wallabies, pademelons, quokkas, and dorcopsis. Wallabies live in a variety of habitats. They range from the rain forests of New Guinea, where the dorcopsis live, to the rocky Australian cliffs where rock wallabies reside.

The yellow-footed rock wallaby is very agile and can leap over 16 feet (5 m).

Tree Kangaroos

There are two species of tree kangaroos living in Australia's rain forests and six species living in New Guinea. These are small to medium-sized kangaroos. They can weigh from 16.5 pounds (7.5 kg) to 33 pounds (15 kg), depending on the species. Tree kangaroos spend most of their time in the trees eating leaves and fruit, coming down only to drink. They have shorter hind legs than most kangaroos, and their forelegs are longer and stronger.

Tree kangaroos, such as the Matschie's kangaroo, move from tree to tree with great ease.

Rat Kangaroos (*Potoroidae*)

This family includes several small species of kangaroos, including musky rat kangaroos, potoroos, and bettongs. These macropods range in size from a rat to a rabbit. They live in areas from arid scrub to wet forest in various parts of Australia. Their diet includes mushrooms, roots, insects, and plants.

Musky Rat Kangaroos

The musky rat kangaroo (*Hypsipymnodon moschatus*) is the smallest kangaroo species. At 14.5 inches (36.8 cm), including their tails, they are no larger than a rat. They also have a bare, rat-like tail and move around on all four feet. Musky rat kangaroos have a four-legged gallop and walk by putting their forepaws on the ground and swinging both hind feet forward. Their basketball-sized nests of leaves are found on the floors of rain forests in northern Australia.

Unlike other kangaroos, the musky rat kangaroo is diurnal, meaning that it is most active during the day.

Potoroos

Potoroos have a pointy nose and mouse-colored fur. They range in size from 13 to 16 inches (33 to 40.6 cm), not including their tail, and weigh from 2.2 to 4.5 pounds (1 to 2 kg). The newly discovered long-footed potoroo (*Potorous longipes*) is the largest of the species. Potoroos live mainly in wet habitats in southeastern and western Australia and Tasmania. Potoroos feed on fungi, roots, and insects. They feed in open areas but need shrubs and ground cover to provide homes and protection.

Although it is small in size, a frightened potoroo can cover almost 8 feet (2.5 m) of ground in a single hop.

Bettongs

Bettongs are the largest members of the potoroid family and can weigh up to 7.7 pounds (3.5 kg). There are four species of bettongs, and most of them are rare because of habitat loss and predators, such as foxes. Bettongs live in drier areas such as the eucalyptus forests and the desert sand hills scattered across Australia. Like the potoroos, they need ground cover and shrub to provide food, homes, and protection. Some species, such as the Tasmanian bettong (*Bettongia gaimardi*), depend on regular bush fires that clear areas. The rare burrowing bettong (*Bettongia lesueur*) is the only kangaroo that regularly digs and lives in burrows.

Like most rat kangaroos, bettongs curl their tails up to carry nest-building materials.

19

Social Activities

Kangaroo social life is affected by whether the climate is dry or wet, what food and shelter are available, and which predators are a threat.

Opposite: Kangaroos usually rest during the day. In the late afternoon, they will become more active and will begin looking for food.

Right: No two kangaroos are exactly alike. Each one has an individual personality.

The kind of environment an animal lives in affects its social activities. Kangaroo social life is affected by whether the climate is dry or wet, what food and shelter are available, and which predators are a threat. Some kangaroos are very social, while others live alone. The behavior of some species, such as the big reds and greys, is quite well known. Other kangaroos have recently been rediscovered and are not well understood. Scientists continue to study different kangaroo species, and we are slowly learning more about their fascinating lives.

Social Groups

Most kangaroos live in groups ranging in size from two or three to about 50. The large kangaroos, such as reds, greys, and some of the larger wallabies, often gather in very large groups. These groups are called **mobs**.

There is safety in numbers. In large, open areas, a mob has more eyes and ears with which to detect predators. Kangaroos living in mobs have less chance of being picked out of the group and eaten.

Most kangaroo mobs have five times as many females as males. Most of the adult females, called does, have young called **joeys** with them. Adult males are called **boomers** and compete with other males for the females. A very strong, old male is called the old man. The old man is **dominant** when it comes to getting food, shade, or mates, but he does not really lead or protect the group. Many females in a mob are related.

Kangaroos also have groups within the mob that they usually associate with more, like having best friends. These kangaroos will spend more time grazing, grooming, and resting together than with other members of the mob, but they remain in sight of the main group for protection.

Some of the smaller kangaroos, such as the quokkas, live in loose family groups, with one male collecting a few females. Other small kangaroos, such as hare wallabies, are solitary, with a usual group consisting of only a mother and a joey.

Kangaroo mobs stay together during times of calm, but at the first sign of danger, they hop off in all directions.

Sparring

Male kangaroos, especially those of the larger species, challenge each other to test their strength. They do this by **sparring**, in what often looks like a boxing match. Two males will rear up on their hind feet and try to push each other off balance. They may jab at each other with their forefeet or lock forelegs as they try to push each other over. They usually throw their heads back to protect their eyes from being scratched. If neither male backs down, the fight may become more intense. The males will aim powerful double-legged kicks at each other. They use their tails to support themselves when they kick.

Fights may occur when a male's access to an individual female or a group of females is challenged.

Usually the males do not injure each other unless the fight turns very serious. The sharp claws on their hind feet are powerful weapons. A well-aimed kick using those claws can rip open the abdomen of an opponent. This weapon is usually reserved for major challenges or as a defense against predators. The skin on the abdomen of male kangaroos is thickened to give protection from this claw.

Many people do not realize that large kangaroos, especially boomers, can be dangerous. If they are harassed or cornered, they will use their hind legs and claws to injure or even kill.

Young male kangaroos start to practice play-sparring at an early age. Their mothers make handy play partners. A young male will wrestle with his mother. He may push her with his front paws and try to knock her over with his hind legs. Mothers are usually tolerant of this behavior.

Communication

Animals of all kinds stay in touch with each other by communicating. Kangaroos, like other animals, have a variety of ways to communicate with one another.

Vocalizations

One way that kangaroos communicate is through vocalizations, which are sounds that send a message. Kangaroos are quiet communicators. Even when frightened, excited, or angry, they do not make loud howls, screams, or snarls. Most vocalizations are made between mothers and joeys or during fights or sparring matches between males. Grunts and clicks can be heard during sparring. Males may use coughing sounds to signal that they want to back away from a fight. Red kangaroo mothers call their joeys with clicking sounds. Grey kangaroo mothers do the same thing with clucks. Both red and grey kangaroos can make a low growling noise when annoyed.

Kangaroos communicate their wants and needs in many ways, including vocalizations.

Body Language

Another way kangaroos communicate is by using their bodies to send signals to each other and to other animals. These signals include foot thumping, kicking, punching, glancing, touching, sniffing, and grooming. Kangaroos may also use signals that we do not yet recognize.

Foot Thumping

A common signal used by kangaroos is the thumping of their large hind feet. This signal always gets attention from others in the group because it signals danger. When the thumping signal is heard, joeys head for their mothers' pouches, and the whole mob scatters in panic.

Sniffing

Many types of kangaroos use sniffing as a way of greeting. Two kangaroos will approach and carefully sniff each other's noses.

Grooming

When grooming, kangaroos lick and comb their own fur and the fur of others. They will use their tongue, their sharp front claws, and the grooming claws on their hind toes. Kangaroos are more likely to groom themselves than to groom other kangaroos. Mother kangaroos groom their young, and females in a mob will sometimes groom each other. Grooming is a friendly gesture that helps keep the animals clean and the group together.

Mutual grooming is considered the height of social harmony in kangaroo society.

Joeys

Kangaroo young spend months developing outside their mother's body in the pouch.

Opposite: A joey continues to nurse even after it has left the pouch.

Kangaroo newborns are very tiny and helpless. If you saw a newborn kangaroo, you would probably not realize that it was a kangaroo. Marsupial animals are born at a much less developed stage than cats, dogs, or humans. Most other mammal young spend months developing inside their mothers' bodies. Kangaroo young spend most of this time developing outside their mother's body in the pouch. While joeys are developing in the pouch, most have an older brother or sister still nursing and a younger one that is ready to develop, waiting in their mother's womb.

Kangaroos raise more young that live to maturity than most other mammals do.

Mating and Birth

Female kangaroos have been described as baby factories. They spend most of their adult lives either pregnant or nursing a joey. Often they do both at the same time, producing one joey after another if the conditions are right. Female kangaroos usually mate with dominant males. These will usually be the older and stronger males. Females may prefer bigger males because their size indicates that they are strong survivors. A kangaroo female does not always mate with the same male, but she will mate with whichever male is dominant in the group. In red kangaroo groups, the old man kangaroo often chases away rival males.

A mother will not let her joey leave her pouch until she has checked the surroundings for danger.

Females will usually mate shortly after they give birth and have a small joey nursing in their pouch. After a female mates, she stores the fertilized egg inside her womb until her joey leaves the pouch. Then, if food and water are available, a new joey will be born. It would not be healthy for the mother or the joey if she gave birth during a **drought**. In dry times when there is not much green food, kangaroos can put off giving birth. The joey will not begin to develop until certain chemicals, found in green food, let the mother's body know it is time for the joey to develop.

Gestation, or the time during which the kangaroo develops in the womb, is very short. Human babies stay in the womb for about 270 days before they are born. Kangaroos are in the womb for only 30 to 40 days.

Care of Young

The bond between mother and joey grows as the youngster develops enough to poke its way out of the pouch. When a foot, a tail, or a nose stick out, the mother will sniff and lick it. After a few months, the joey will stick its head out and inspect the world while its mother hops around. During this time the joey depends on its mother for food, warmth, protection, and transportation. The mother carries the joey with her everywhere. Without her, it is unlikely the little kangaroo would survive. No other group member helps raise the joey.

As the joey gets bigger, it starts to leave the pouch and begins to eat grass. By watching what its mother eats, the joey learns to **forage**. Even as the joey gets almost too big for the pouch, it continues to return to its mother to nurse and for comfort. By this time it probably has a small brother or sister in the pouch.

Older joeys that are out of the pouch have to watch out for eagles, dingoes, large lizards, and snakes. If the mother spots danger, she warns the joey with a thump of her foot or another sound. The joey dives back into the pouch headfirst, and the mother draws her pouch muscles closed to seal off the entrance. If a female kangaroo is chased and she has a large joey in her pouch, she may deliberately dump the joey out in tall grass or shrubs where it can hide. She can then escape because she is able to run faster with a lighter load. If she is caught with a joey in her pouch, it is likely they would both die.

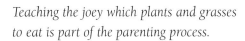

Teaching the joey which plants and grasses to eat is part of the parenting process.

Development

Birth to 3 Months

Newborns are blind, deaf, and hairless. Only their tiny head, shoulders, and forearms are formed. As soon as they are born, they must crawl up their mother's furry abdomen into the pouch. They use their arms like paddles through water to pull themselves into the pouch. This is a distance of about 6 inches (15.2 cm). If the tiny joey cannot find the pouch within a few minutes, it can die from exposure. The mother may lick a trail to the pouch, but she will not guide the joey in any other way. The joey is likely guided to the pouch by the smell of milk. Once in the pouch, the joey will begin to nurse. It will stay in this position for several months as it grows and develops.

A joey does not develop fur until it is almost 6 months old.

3 to 6 Months

Big changes begin for the joey when it is about 15 weeks old. The milk it drinks becomes richer, with more fat and protein. It is time for the joey to start growing. A tail has grown, and the baby claws are well formed. By 17 weeks of age, the joey's eyes have opened. The ears have opened as well, but they are folded back against the head. The joey is still pink-skinned and hairless for most of this time.

6 to 9 Months

When the joey reaches 6 months of age, its mother's milk becomes even richer with a high fat content. By 6 months the young kangaroo can better control its body temperature and has a coat of fur. During this time the joey will often stick its head out of the pouch to look around. It may even nibble on grass as its mother grazes. Mother and joey start to form a close bond. The mother regularly cleans the pouch and joey by licking them.

9 to 18 Months

By the time the joey is 9 months old, it will be able to leave the pouch and explore the outside world. The young kangaroo is curious and has much to learn. It learns to eat grasses and other plants by watching its mother. The joey licks saliva from its mother's mouth. This helps them to bond. The mother's saliva passes on tiny bacteria that help the joey digest the green plant food. The joey still returns to the pouch for milk and comfort. By 1 year old, it is too big for the pouch but sticks its head in the pouch for an occasional drink of milk.

18+ Months

By this time the young kangaroo is no longer dependent on its mother. A young female may start to mate soon and have joeys of her own. Young males practice sparring with other young males. They need to grow larger and put on more weight before they can interest a female kangaroo as a mate.

A joey's first trip out of the pouch can be a bit wobbly. Once it finds its footing, however, the joey will be in and out of the pouch on a regular basis.

Habitat

In some areas kangaroos have become quite specialized to cope with the conditions in which they live.

Some kangaroos live in dry, desert environments (opposite), while others, such as the quokka (below), frequent moist, swamp areas.

The continent of Australia has many habitats. Kangaroos have spread out to occupy almost every type of habitat. In some areas they have become quite specialized to cope with the conditions in which they live.

Kangaroos have a long history in Australia. While kangaroos are still found in every part of the country, they often reside in scattered pockets due to habitat loss. Some of the large kangaroos have taken advantage of habitat changes made by humans and have expanded their range. These changes tend to benefit only the large species. The habitat of small forest dwellers is disappearing.

Kangaroos and the Ecosystem

All of the animals and plants in a given habitat form an ecosystem. The ecosystem is a web of relationships between living creatures in a specific environment. These relationships can be complicated. Removing or changing one part of the ecosystem can upset the whole balance.

Kangaroos play an important role in their ecosystems. In 1978 two small kangaroos were caught in a cage trap in southeastern Australia. They were a male and a female of a new species of potoroo. Potoroos are small kangaroos that live in the dense shrubbery of wet forests. This particular species had never been seen alive and was named the long-footed potoroo.

These long-footed potoroos live only in small pockets of rain forest in the Australian states of Victoria and New South Wales. Their main food source is underground fungi, and they spread the fungi's spores in their feces. Scientists now know these fungi provide nutrients that trees in the forest need to grow. The long-footed potoroo is a crucial link in the health of the rain forest. This shy little kangaroo has now become a symbol for people who are fighting to stop the logging of forests in southeastern Australia. These people have a newsletter called the *Potoroo Review*.

Kangaroos and their habitats are equally dependent on each other.

Which Kangaroo Are You?

Using what you have learned so far in this book, try to match the kangaroo clue with the correct type of kangaroo.

1 Pointy nose and mouse-colored fur

2 Shorter hind legs than most kangaroos

3 Has a nail-like tip on the end of the tail

4 Lives on rocky Australian cliffs

5 Have pouches for their young

6 Smallest kangaroo species

A Rock wallaby

B Tree kangaroo

C All kangaroos

D Potoroo

E Musky rat kangaroo

F Nail-tail wallaby

Answers: 1. D. Potoroo 2. B. Tree kangaroo 3. F. Nail-tail wallaby 4. A. Rock wallaby 5. C. All kangaroos 6. E. Musky rat kangaroo

Food

Grasses are the plants most commonly eaten by kangaroos.

Opposite: Almost all of a kangaroo's waking hours are spent eating.

Right: To find food, rat kangaroos use their front paws to turn over leaves and small rocks.

Most kangaroos are plant-eaters, so they belong to the group of animals called **herbivores**. Grasses are the plants most commonly eaten by kangaroos. Some of the smaller forest kangaroos are browsers. That means they eat leaves, twigs, and bark off trees and shrubs. To eat, they sit up and hold their food in their forepaws.

Rat kangaroos, potoroos, and bettongs have different diets. Many of them eat mushrooms and other fungi. Insects also form a part of their diet.

Kangaroos dig holes to find water and to stay cool. As the ground underneath the topsoil is normally cooler, kangaroos sometimes use the holes they have dug as resting spots.

Water

Like all living things, kangaroos need water to survive. Kangaroos that live in dry areas may get all the water they need from the plants they eat. Many species have developed ways of saving water in their bodies. They do not sweat very much, and their urine and feces contain very little water. They spend the hottest part of the day resting in the shade and are active mainly in the cooler evening and night. Some desert-dwelling rock wallabies are so good at saving water that they never need to drink. One species, the tammar wallaby, can drink sea water, something few other mammals can do.

Most kangaroos can go without water for a while but still welcome it when it is available. Some kangaroos dig deep holes that collect underground water. Kangaroos that live on farmland often take advantage of water set out for sheep and cattle.

How Do Kangaroos Eat?

Kangaroos spend a large part of their time eating, chewing, and digesting their food. They eat by putting their forelegs down on the ground and bending over. Once in position, they swing their head from side to side, snipping off all the grass stems within reach. When kangaroos have been grazing in an area, it can look like a lawnmower has cut the grass.

Plant material, especially tough grasses, contains **cellulose**. This is the material that makes plants stiff. It is very difficult to digest. Kangaroos have to eat plenty of grass to survive because grass does not contain many nutrients. The animals have to break down the cellulose so that they can digest the food and get the maximum amount of energy from it. They eat slowly to be sure their food is finely ground before swallowing. When they swallow, the food goes to their stomach. Millions of special bacteria live in a kangaroo's stomach. The bacteria turn cellulose into energy. Without the bacteria, kangaroos would not be able to get enough nutrients out of their food.

Grass is so low in calories that kangaroos must eat huge quantities of it just to stay alive.

The Food Cycle

A food cycle shows how energy, in the form of food, is passed from one living thing to another. Kangaroos are herbivores because they get their food energy from eating plants. Meat-eating animals, called carnivores, get some of their food energy by eating kangaroos and other animals. Kangaroos affect the lives of many other creatures in the food cycle.

Predators such as dingoes, Tasmanian devils, and even eagles can prey on kangaroos.

Bacteria make their home in the kangaroo's stomach. They help the kangaroo digest its food.

Other animals use the water holes dug by kangaroos.

Kangaroos are herbivores that get energy from eating fungi and plants, such as grasses and shrubs.

Feces from kangaroos can help spread plant seeds and fungi spores in the environment.

Kangaroos and other animals that die provide food for scavengers and nutrients for the soil. These nutrients help plants grow.

Wildlife Biologists Talk About Kangaroos

Dr. David Croft

"Tourists should see kangaroos in the wild, but instead they see them in a zoo or dead by the side of a road. If we can find areas with large kangaroo populations and develop them properly, kangaroos will become a positive tourist attraction. This will also encourage farmers to see kangaroos as a benefit rather than as a pest."

David Croft teaches at the University of New South Wales and is one of Australia's foremost experts on kangaroo behavior and biology.

Lynette Campbell

"If kangaroos are used for meat, for fur, for leather, then that's all people will see. People won't recognize their...value as wildlife, as animals in their own right beyond the realm of the human world. Everything is linked together and if we damage this species we're damaging ourselves."

Lynette Campbell is a scientist who has been actively involved in the rescue, rehabilitation, and release of orphaned joeys whose mothers have died as a result of car accidents or hunting. Her work was featured on the video "Kangaroos," which was part of the *Champions in the Wild* television series.

Graeme Moss

"The brush-tailed rock wallaby's status is currently listed as threatened within New South Wales. Wallaby populations are being monitored on the mountain peaks at the Warrumbungle National Park [where] goats and foxes are potential threats.... This will [result] in the development of an improved recovery plan for the wallabies in the park."

Graeme Moss teaches wildlife ecology at the University of New England in New South Wales. He has written articles on several kangaroo species, especially the red kangaroo. He is a consultant to the New South Wales National Parks and Wildlife Service.

Competition

Introduced animals form some of the heaviest competition kangaroos face.

Even in Australia's wide open spaces, kangaroos find themselves in competition with many other creatures. They compete with other kangaroos for food, water, shelter, and mates.

Dingoes hunt kangaroos of most sizes. Smaller marsupial predators, such as the Tasmanian devil, can kill small kangaroo species. Unwary young kangaroos that stray too far from their mothers' pouches can be eaten by eagles and large lizards. Humans also hunt and kill kangaroos for food and leather, and to eliminate them as competitors to their cattle and sheep. Many other animals introduced to Australia by humans, such as cats, dogs, goats, foxes, and rabbits, either kill kangaroos or compete with them for food. These introduced animals form some of the heaviest competition kangaroos face.

Opposite: As kangaroos use their ears to listen for danger, predators, such as dingoes, have a better chance of success when hunting from a down-wind postion.

Right: The Tasmanian devil has the greatest jaw strength of almost any other animal.

Competition with Other Kangaroos

The kangaroo is a timid animal. It will not attack unless it is provoked.

Within large mobs of kangaroos, competition between males can be stiff. The play-sparring that joeys learn helps them compete when they are older. The larger and more dominant boomers have the biggest selection of females for mating. Smaller or weaker males may not find a mate at all. The old man kangaroo may chase most or all rival males out of the group.

When a kangaroo mob grazes on a large area, its members may not have to compete for food. If food is scarce or found only in scattered areas, they will have to compete to get enough food. This can happen in a drought or after a fire. Kangaroos may compete over who gets to drink first at a water source or who gets the best shade spots if these are scarce.

Relationships with Other Animals

Kangaroos may also have to compete with other animals for food and places to live. In many areas kangaroo habitats are shrinking because other species of animals are moving in. These other species are often animals introduced to Australia by humans, such as rabbits, mice, and goats. These animals have done well in their new environment and have spread rapidly. They often take over the habitats of kangaroos and can out-compete the kangaroos. They eat the kangaroos' food and use or destroy their living spaces.

Kangaroos can also have problems with predators that have been brought to Australia by humans. The dingo was the first to arrive, about 3,000 years ago. More recent arrivals that are causing serious problems for kangaroos are **feral** cats, dogs, and foxes. Small kangaroos are especially vulnerable to these predators. Kangaroos evolved in a land where there were few ground-dwelling predators and have not developed defenses against them. Native predators, such as the marsupial wolf and marsupial tiger, have not been seen for years. They could not compete with newcomers to their land.

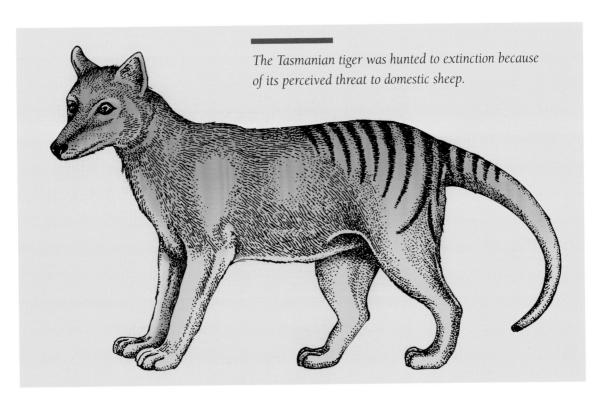

The Tasmanian tiger was hunted to extinction because of its perceived threat to domestic sheep.

Competition from Humans

As more European settlers came to Australia over the last few hundred years, they increasingly affected the lives of kangaroos and other marsupials. Kangaroos not only had to share their food, but also often became food for humans and certain introduced species.

Kangaroos and humans experience the most conflict on farmlands. Humans have put up fences to keep their livestock on their land and to protect them. Still, these fences rarely keep kangaroos from traveling to reach food and water sources. Humans often consider kangaroos to be pests that eat the grass needed for their sheep and cattle. Yet, researchers have found that kangaroos normally prefer to eat different grasses than sheep do. The two can often graze side by side without really competing. However, in times of drought, kangaroos have fewer choices, and they can move in on grass intended for livestock.

Smaller kangaroos also have to compete with humans for living space. Many areas in which they live, including swamps, forests, plains, and woodlands, are being turned into housing developments, towns, and farms. Many species of small kangaroos are being pushed out of their habitats, with nowhere to go.

Overgrazing by kangaroos, domestic livestock, and feral animals has a negative effect on other animals as well as on plant species and soil.

Viewpoints

Is it acceptable to remove problem animals in order to save kangaroos?

Many kangaroos are having a hard time surviving because of the animals that have been introduced into Australia. Huge numbers of rabbits, mice, and goats eat kangaroo food and destroy their habitat. Some feral cats and foxes use the smaller kangaroos as food. Many solutions have been tried to get rid of these animals. Some of these involve releasing diseased animals that will kill other animals of the same species. Millions of rabbits have been killed in this way. Other methods of control include trapping, shooting, or poisoning large numbers of rabbits, foxes, and cats.

PRO

1 These introduced animals are destroying Australia's natural wildlife heritage. Once the kangaroos become extinct, they will never return. Drastic methods must be used to save them.

2 Many of these pest animals, such as rabbits and mice, also destroy crops and pastures. The livelihoods of farmers have to be protected.

3 The numbers of pest animals are growing so rapidly that there is no time to find more humane methods of removing them.

CON

1 It is unacceptable to treat some animals inhumanely in order to protect others.

2 Some methods of removing pest animals, such as poisoning or disease, may affect kangaroos and other native animals in ways we do not yet understand.

3 Many problems for kangaroos are caused by habitat loss from farms raising sheep and cattle. Nothing is being done to control the effects of these introduced animals.

Folklore

Kangaroos have an important place in the legends and folklore of the Australian **Aborigines**, who were the first people to encounter kangaroos at least 40,000 years ago. When European explorers first came to Australia, they were amazed by the strange hopping creatures with their pouches and huge feet. It is said that the kangaroos received their name when baffled explorers asked the Aborigines what these strange creatures were. As the story goes, the Aborigines themselves were baffled by these strange new people. They answered, "I don't understand what you mean." Their word for this was "kangaroo." The explorers took this to be the creature's name, and that name has stuck ever since. Historians argue that there is no proof that this tale is true, but it is a part of the folklore surrounding kangaroos.

Opposite: In the early 1900s, people sometimes put boxing gloves on male red or grey kangaroos and had them box humans. Kangaroos did not have to be trained how to hit, as this was part of their normal behavior. Most people now believe this activity was cruel. It used a kangaroo's natural behavior in a way that could cause the animal stress and injury.

Kanga is a popular character in A.A. Milne's Winnie-the-Pooh *series.*

Folklore History

Kangaroos have appeared in the legends of the Australian people for thousands of years. Their stories have been told from one generation to another. Their legends and stories have also been recorded in rock paintings and drawings. Many of these are very ancient and considered sacred.

An ancient Aboriginal legend tells of how the first kangaroos came to live in Australia. According to the legend, there was a huge windstorm that blew strange-looking creatures through the air. The animals struggled to reach the ground. They stretched their legs so much in their efforts to touch down that their back legs grew very long. When they finally dropped to the ground, they hopped away on their new long legs.

Kangaroos are featured in many of the Aboriginal folktales of Australia.

Myths vs. Facts

Kangaroos in a mob are all the same.

Kangaroos have been seen communicating and relating to each other, and were all easily recognizable as unique individuals.

Using a pouch to raise young is an inferior way of reproducing.

Some researchers think that marsupial reproduction may be the best way to produce young in the dry and often harsh conditions found in Australia.

Large male kangaroos like to fight and are natural boxers.

Large male kangaroos use sparring behavior to compete with other male kangaroos for mates and other things that they need to survive. They also use it as a way of defending themselves against predators. They do not look for fights with other animals and are not aggressive when left alone.

Folktales

There have been many fascinating folktales and stories written and told about kangaroos. Many of these deal with the kangaroo's unique characteristics, especially its legs and its hopping abilities. Folktales about kangaroos are often tied closely to the Aboriginal experience of the land and their relationship to the animals that live on it. Here are a few folktales and stories about kangaroos. You can probably find more at your library.

Strange Friends

The legend "A Strange Friendship" deals with a friendship between a little bird called Willie Wagtail and a red kangaroo named Miru. Miru, the red kangaroo, was strong and could fight. Willie Wagtail could sing beautifully. Each envied the other's abilities and tried to imitate the other, which almost destroyed their friendship. Then, danger threatened, and the little bird and the big kangaroo learned a valuable lesson about the importance of sharing skills and working together.

Morgan, Sally. *The Flying Emu and Other Australian Stories.* New York: Alfred A. Knopf, 1992.

The Old Man

The unique adventures of Old Man Kangaroo come to life in this classic "Just So Story." In this tale from long ago, Old Man Kangaroo's legs were all one length, and his fur was gray and woolly. Old Man Kangaroo looked quite ordinary, but he wanted to look special and be popular with the other creatures. He visited the god Nqong to make his request and got more than he bargained for.

Kipling, Rudyard. *The Sing-Song of Old Man Kangaroo.* New York: Harper & Row, 1986.

Hopping About

"The Legs of the Kangaroo" is an
Aboriginal legend about the kangaroo's
legs. When Kangaroo first arrived on the
canoe of Whale, he had legs equal in
length. Once in Australia, Kangaroo met
Man for the first time. Man had long
tireless legs and dangerous weapons. Man
chased Kangaroo all day, and when night
fell he lit a fire. In order to hide from the
firelight, Kangaroo rose up on his tiptoes
to sneak away. In his haste to get away,
Kangaroo stayed on two legs. Kangaroo
liked the sensation and experimented with
it, until he found a way of traveling on
two legs that was fast and covered great
distances. He has been hopping that way
ever since.

Myths, Legends and Fables. Reed Interactive:
  <www.ozemail.com.au/~reed/
  global/kanga.html>

Dreamtime Animals

In this story, a boy learns from his elders
how animals created a world in which
they could all live in peace and harmony.
As the story goes, long ago in the time
called Dreamtime, Earth was watery and
unformed. Then, the Great Ancestor gave
life to all the four-legged, winged, and
gilled animals. The animals fought with
each other as they searched for a place
to live. Finally Garn-dag-ity the kangaroo,
the emu, and the long-necked turtle
began to dream. In their dreams Earth
took firm shape, making many different
homes for the animals. Since then,
animals have shared Earth.

Morin, Paul. *Animal Dreaming: An
  Aboriginal Dreamtime*. Toronto:
  Stoddart Kids, 1998.

Kangaroo Distribution

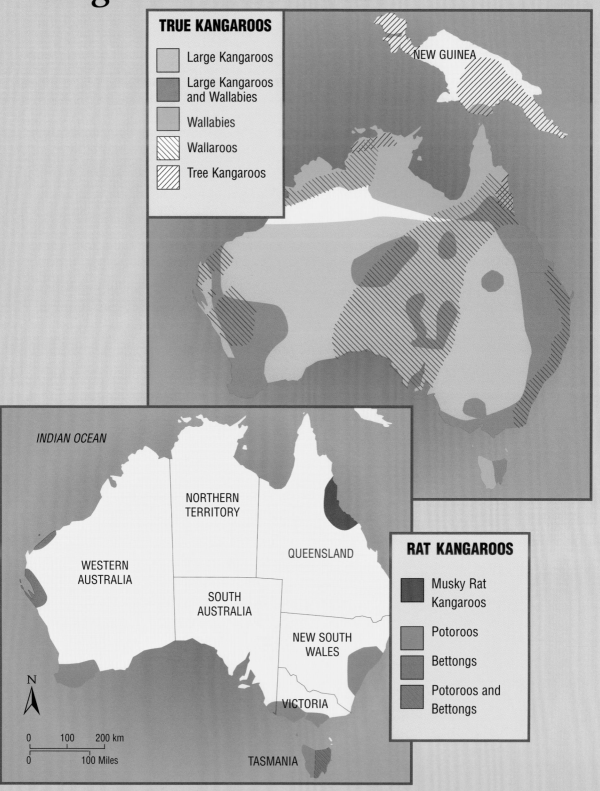

TRUE KANGAROOS

- Large Kangaroos
- Large Kangaroos and Wallabies
- Wallabies
- Wallaroos
- Tree Kangaroos

NEW GUINEA

INDIAN OCEAN

NORTHERN TERRITORY

QUEENSLAND

WESTERN AUSTRALIA

SOUTH AUSTRALIA

NEW SOUTH WALES

VICTORIA

TASMANIA

RAT KANGAROOS

- Musky Rat Kangaroos
- Potoroos
- Bettongs
- Potoroos and Bettongs

N

| 0 | 100 | 200 km |

| 0 | 100 Miles |

Status

Many kangaroos, especially some of the smaller species, are threatened and could soon become extinct.

Opposite: Kangaroos can be found all over Australia and Tasmania, as well as in parts of New Guinea.

Right: The bridled nail-tail wallaby is one of Australia's endangered kangaroo species.

There are about 53 to 69 known species of kangaroos in Australia. At least six species have become extinct in the past 200 years. This was when Europeans started to settle in Australia. Many other kangaroo species, especially some of the smaller ones, are threatened and could soon become extinct. Those in greatest danger are the tree kangaroos, hare wallabies, nail-tail wallabies, some of the rock wallabies, and many of the small forest species, such as potoroos and bettongs. For these species, the changes to their habitats have been too great for their survival. In many cases, their habitats have almost completely disappeared. Heavy hunting and too many new predators have also taken their toll.

Some of the larger species have done better. The grey and red kangaroos have actually grown in number and extended their range in some areas. These kangaroos take advantage of the grass and water intended for farm animals.

Threats to Kangaroos

Even though kangaroos are protected from hunting by laws in Australia, the government issues permits to hunt some kangaroos where they occur in large numbers. Licensed "shooters" go out at night and kill a predetermined number of kangaroos. The shooters prefer to take the bigger males because they provide more meat and hides. Some people believe this to be the best way to handle the surplus kangaroos. If there are too many kangaroos in an area, they may starve in times of drought, or they may compete

Bettongs are small animals that may not be visible from a fast-moving car.

with livestock to get enough food. Others think it is a bad practice. They worry that too many kangaroos may be killed in this way. If females are killed, the joeys in their pouches will also die.

Changing fire patterns have also posed a threat to kangaroo habitats. The small brush fires that Aborigines often set used to provide new habitat for kangaroos. These fires ensured that small areas of land would regenerate each year. Now that these small fires have declined, large and dangerous wildfires have increased because of the build-up of brush in the woodlands and forests. Large fires destroy too much kangaroo habitat, forcing the animals to travel far to find new places to live.

A third danger comes from cars. Most large kangaroos are most active at dawn and dusk. This is why many kangaroos are hit by cars and killed each year. At night, the kangaroos' eyes shine in the reflection of headlights, making the animals easier to detect. In the day, if they are moving, they are easily visible. Since light is low at dusk and dawn, and headlights are not as effective, it is difficult to see kangaroos along the side of the road.

Extinct Species Rediscovered

Australia is a large country, and some kangaroo habitat falls within areas that are difficult to access. Many of the smaller species of kangaroos are secretive and protect themselves by hiding. Some species of kangaroos that were once thought to be extinct have recently been rediscovered. Although these animals seem to have come back from extinction, they are still endangered and need to be protected.

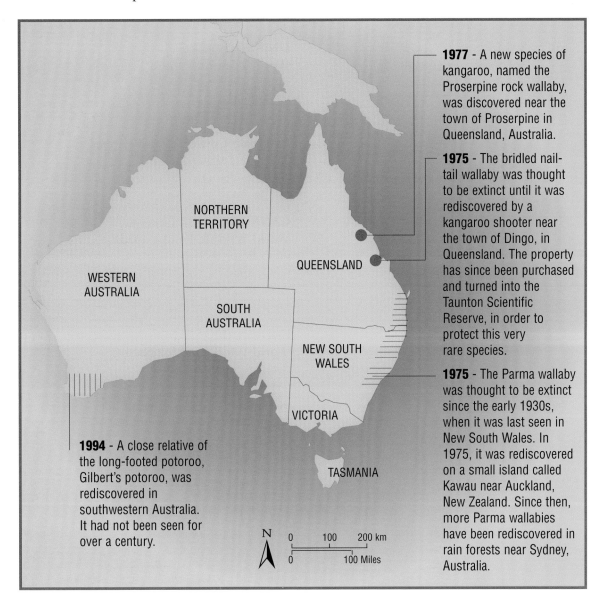

1977 - A new species of kangaroo, named the Proserpine rock wallaby, was discovered near the town of Proserpine in Queensland, Australia.

1975 - The bridled nail-tail wallaby was thought to be extinct until it was rediscovered by a kangaroo shooter near the town of Dingo, in Queensland. The property has since been purchased and turned into the Taunton Scientific Reserve, in order to protect this very rare species.

1975 - The Parma wallaby was thought to be extinct since the early 1930s, when it was last seen in New South Wales. In 1975, it was rediscovered on a small island called Kawau near Auckland, New Zealand. Since then, more Parma wallabies have been rediscovered in rain forests near Sydney, Australia.

1994 - A close relative of the long-footed potoroo, Gilbert's potoroo, was rediscovered in southwestern Australia. It had not been seen for over a century.

NORTHERN TERRITORY

WESTERN AUSTRALIA

QUEENSLAND

SOUTH AUSTRALIA

NEW SOUTH WALES

VICTORIA

TASMANIA

N

0   100   200 km

0   100 Miles

What You Can Do

Kangaroos are fascinating creatures that need your help. You can learn more about kangaroos by writing to a conservation organization for more information.

Conservation Groups

AUSTRALIA
The New South Wales Wildlife Information and Rescue Service (WIRES)
247–251 Flinders Lane
Melbourne, VIC
3000

Noah's Ark Wildlife Coalition
P.O. Box 1249
Beenleigh, QLD
4207

Threatened Species Network World Wildlife Fund
Australia, Sydney Office
GPO Box 528
Sydney, NSW
2001

The Kangaroo Protection Cooperative
GPO Box 3719
Sydney, NSW
2001

UNITED STATES
World Wildlife Fund U.S.
1250 24th Street NW
Washington, DC
20037

Kangaroo Conservation Center
222 Bailey-Waters Road
Dawsonville, GA
30534

CANADA
World Wildlife Fund Canada
90 Eglinton Avenue E.
Suite 504
Toronto, ON
M4P 2Z7

INTERNATIONAL
World Wide Fund for Nature
Avenue du Mont Blanc
CH-1196 Gland
Switzerland

Twenty Fascinating Facts

1 Fast-traveling kangaroos remain in the air about 70 to 80 percent of the time.

2 Although kangaroos are nocturnal, some rock wallabies bask in the sun during the day.

3 The sprint-hop of a large kangaroo at 40 miles per hour (64 km/h) is faster than a racehorse can run.

4 In a kangaroo mob, females outnumber males five to one.

5 Some species of desert-living rock wallabies are so adapted to dry conditions that they never need to drink. They survive on the water in the plants they eat and lose very little water in their urine or feces.

6 Swamp wallabies make chemicals in their livers that protect them from deadly poisons in some of the plants they eat, such as orchids.

7 The western grey kangaroo is sometimes nicknamed "Stinker." Large males of this species smell like curry.

8 Most species of kangaroos never stop growing throughout their lives.

9 The musky rat kangaroo is the only kangaroo that does not use hopping as its main form of locomotion.

10 Kangaroos are excellent swimmers.

11 Several species of small kangaroos have tails that can wrap around and carry twigs and grass with them for nesting material. When they need to hide or rest, they have a ready-made nest.

12 A joey is so firmly attached to its milk source during the first few months of life that it stays in place even when its mother is hopping about at a great speed. If it gets dislodged, it can find its way back.

13 Thirsty kangaroos have been known to dig holes 4 feet (1 m) deep to find water. Other animals then use these kangaroo-created wells to help them through the dry seasons.

14 If danger threatens an older joey, it will dive headfirst into its mother's pouch, doing a complete somersault to face the opening. The mother then contracts her pouch muscles to seal the opening.

15 Nail-tail wallabies have a unique habit of moving their forelegs in circles when they hop. This has earned them the nickname "organ-grinders."

16 Kangaroos can jump huge distances when moving fast but use less energy while doing it. They are the only animals that use less energy the faster they travel.

17 Unlike other kangaroos, musky rat kangaroos often give birth to twins.

18 Kangaroos have a habit of hopping away quickly from danger and then stopping to look around. This makes them an easy target for hunters.

19 Dorcopsis have a habit of placing only the tips of their tails on the forest floor when resting. This may be to keep their tails away from leeches. Pademelons, who also live in rain forests, keep their tails on the ground. The underside of their tails often have leeches attached.

20 The record for distance leaping goes to a male grey kangaroo that jumped 44 feet (13.4 m) in a single leap. This is longer than a large school bus.

Glossary

Aborigines: The first people to live in Australia, who inhabited the country about 40,000 years before the European explorers

boomers: Adult male kangaroos, especially of the large species

cellulose: Material found in plants that makes them stiff

dingo: A species of wild dog found in Australia

dominant: An animal that is more powerful and has a higher rank than others in the group

drought: A long period without rain

feral: A domestic animal, such as a dog or cat, that lives in the wild and cares for itself

forage: To search for food

gestation: The time a female is pregnant

herbivores: Animals that eat only plants

joeys: Young kangaroos

macropods: Marsupial animals that move on two large hind legs

mammals: Warm-blooded animals that breathe air and nurse their young

marsupials: Mammals that give birth to undeveloped young; many marsupials carry their developing young in a pouch in their body

mob: A group of many kangaroos that live together

sparring: Hitting and pushing with forelegs. Sparring resembles human boxing.

tendons: Tissues that attach muscle to bone

Suggested Reading

Brust, B.W. *Kangaroos*. Mankato, MN: Creative Education Inc., 1991.

Burt, D. *Kangaroos*. Boston: Houghton Mifflin, 1991.

Darling, K. & T. *Kangaroos on Location*. New York: Lothrop, Lee & Shepard, 1993.

Dawson, T. J. *Kangaroos: Biology of the Largest Marsupials*. Ithaca: Cornell University Press, 1995.

Domico, T. *Kangaroos: The Marvelous Mob*. New York: Facts on File, 1993.

Markle, S. *Outside and Inside Kangaroos*. New York: Atheneum, 1999.

KANGAROOS ON THE INTERNET

One of the places you can find out more about kangaroos is on the Internet. Visit the following sites, or try searching on your own:

Australian Wildlife
http://www.australianwildlife.com.au/features/kangaroo.htm

Kangaroo Conservation Center
http://www.kangaroocenter.com./index.html

National Wildlife Federation
http://www.nwf.org/internationalwildlife/kangaroo.html

Index